Best of
LONDON

UNICHROME A Unichrome Publication

Best of
LONDON

Contents

Written and edited by Angela Royston.
Designed by Aardvark Design Studio Ltd.
Front cover designed by John Buckley.
Picture research by Jan Kean.
The publishers would like to thank Peter Matthews for reading the text.

Acknowledgements:
Photography © Pitkin Unichrome by Steve Day.
Additional photography by kind permission of the following:
British Museum: p46L
Collections: (Liba Taylor) p43CR, p 44/45
Colorsport: p43B, p44BL
Dee Conway: p50BR
Alan Copson: p12B, p15TC, p27CR, p28/29, p30/31B, p40BL, p52/53T, p54T&BR, p56/57, p59BR, p60/61T&B, p61CR, p61BR, p63C
Crown Copyright/Her Majesty's Stationery Office: p32T
Dean & Chapter of Westminster: p14/15
Mark Fiennes: p16/17T
Tim Graham: p45CR
Robert Harding: (Adam Woolfitt) p43L
The Impact Agency: p62/63B
Pawel Libera: p12T, p20/21, p24 all, p31BR, p42B, p51B, p57TC, p62T, p63BR
London Zoo: p5TL
Mary Evans Picture Library: p6/7, p9C, p10/11
Museum of London: p6BL, p7TR, p47BR
National Gallery, London: p48B
National Maritime Museum, London: p37BR
Natural History Museum: p47TL
Pitkin Unichrome: p15C&BR, p16BL, p33TL, p41B, p45BR
Pitkin Unichrome: (Heather Hook) p5, p11C, p25BR, p33CR&BR, p36B, p37CR, p52BL, p56BL
Pitkin Unichrome: (Mark Slade) p13TL, p14L, p18T&BL, p18/19, p44TL, p57BR
Richmond-Upon-Thames Borough Council: p42T
The Royal Collection © HM Queen Elizabeth II: p13TR
Robert Royston: p36T, p38TL, p50T, p58BR, p59TL, p59CR
Tate Gallery, London: p49B
V & A Picture Library: p47BL

Printed in Singapore.
ISBN 1 871004 72 1 (hardback) 1/00
ISBN 1 871004 73 X (paperback) 1/00

FS 32611
Pitkin Unichrome is a publishing, design and photographic company registered to ISO 9001 by the British Standards Institution.

For most of its 2,000-year history, London has been an important trading city and the centre of political and royal power. Trade brought in people and goods from across the world, making London, from its very beginning, a wealthy, cosmopolitan city; its importance as a political capital gave rise to fine buildings, monuments and royal ceremonial.

Evidence of London's Roman past frequently comes to light when the foundations for new buildings are excavated. This Roman tombstone is from the Museum of London.

The Romans

Small settlements of people had lived on the marshy banks of the Thames since the Stone Age, but it was the Romans who built the first city. As they marched north from Kent in AD 43, their engineers saw that the gravel banks each side of the present London Bridge, where the swampy river narrowed, made an ideal crossing point. A bridge was built and the Roman city of Londinium was established as a port and trading post for the Roman empire.

Less than 20 years later, Boudicca, queen of the Iceni tribe, attacked and burned the new settlement (and Colchester and St Albans too) in revenge for mistreatment by the Romans, but the disciplined Roman army defeated her forces. A statue of Boudicca stands on the Embankment, opposite London Eye.

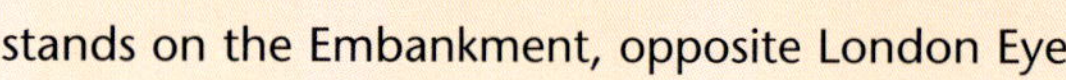

Londinium was rebuilt and by AD 100 had become the capital of the Roman province. Goods were brought in from all parts of the empire, and corn, pewter, silver and other materials shipped back to Rome. A massive stone wall was built around Londinium, sections of which can still be seen at London Wall and on the north side of the Tower of London. The Roman Empire came under increasing attack across Europe and, in AD 410, the Romans retreated, the buildings crumbled and the wharves silted up.

Saxons and Danes

After the Romans withdrew from Britain, waves of invaders took over, including Saxons from Germany and Vikings from Denmark and Norway. The main part of the Saxon city, called Lundenwic, was to the west of the Roman city, around the Strand, but the area of the old Roman city again became a landing-place for ships and a centre for trade. On high ground between them,

In medieval times London Bridge was made of stone and densely packed with wooden shops and houses. It remained the only bridge across the Thames until 1750.

King Ethelbert, the first English king to convert to Christianity, founded St Paul's Cathedral in 604.

According to legend, a church was also established further up the Thames at what is now Westminster. But it was not until the 11th century that King Edward, nicknamed 'the Confessor' because he was so pious, allocated a tenth of his wealth to build a magnificent church at 'West Minster'. He built a new royal palace next to the site and moved his court there, so establishing the centre of political power at Westminster, where it remains today, outside the City.

The Normans

William the Conqueror was crowned in Westminster Abbey on Christmas Day 1066 and soon made his mark on London. The White Tower, the central keep of the Tower of London, was completed in about 1097. His son added a great hall – Westminster Hall – to the palace at Westminster. It is now part of the Houses of Parliament and the only part of the original royal palace to survive.

William's successors granted London many privileges, which the area known as the City retains today, including the right to elect its own Lord Mayor and govern itself. When the first mayor was elected in 1192, trade was flourishing and the first stone bridge was being built across the river at London Bridge.

Medieval London

In medieval London, manors, religious houses, churches, quays and narrow streets of houses all jostled for space within the original Roman walls. The most powerful groups in the city were the livery companies or craft guilds that provided hospitals, chapels and meeting halls for their members and regulated and protected their craft.

To the west of the city walls (on the south side of Fleet Street) lawyers and law students leased property from the Knights Hospitallers to found two of London's four Inns of Court.

The Guildhall in the City dates from 1411, although much of it was rebuilt after the Great Fire of London and the Blitz.

Tudor Times

During the 16th century London's population quadrupled from 50,000 to 200,000, the extra people spilling into areas around the City. Henry VIII had several palaces along the Thames and travelled up and down the river by boat, from Eltham and Greenwich to Westminster, Richmond or, most magnificent of all, Hampton Court. A keen hunter, Henry enclosed large tracts of land as deer parks, including what are now St James's Park and Hyde Park.

The Tower of London has witnessed many horrific events, especially during the reigns of the Tudors: the executions of two of Henry VIII's six wives – Anne Boleyn and Catherine Howard – and those who defied him, including Sir Thomas More. Even Elizabeth I spent some time in the Tower as a prisoner of her sister Queen Mary before acceding to the throne of England.

London's first theatre, 'The Theatre', opened in Shoreditch in 1576, just a few years before William Shakespeare came to London. To escape censorship by the City's Lord Mayor, the Rose and Globe theatres were rebuilt south of the river, in Southwark, in an area then largely occupied by bear pits, prisons and brothels. Today Shakespeare's Globe has been meticulously reconstructed close to the site of the original theatre.

The Stuarts

When James VI of Scotland came to London to become James I of Scotland and England, he found a city bustling with enterprise and activity. Hackney carriages – horse-drawn London taxis – first appeared in about 1625 and quickly became so successful their number was limited to 400 in 1661 to control congestion.

James I appointed Inigo Jones as the King's Surveyor. One of his earliest projects was the building of the Queen's House at Greenwich, which, like the Banqueting House in Whitehall, still stands today.

When Charles I became embroiled in a struggle for power with parliament, London took the side of Oliver Cromwell and the Parliamentarians. The defeated king was tried for treason in Westminster Hall and executed outside the Banqueting House. Nevertheless 11 years later, in 1660, London welcomed the restoration of the monarchy and the accession of Charles II.

Shortly afterwards, two disasters befell London, both recorded and described by the diarist Samuel Pepys. In 1665 the Great Plague – recurrent since the 14th century – killed 100,000 people, and the following year the Great Fire destroyed nearly four-fifths of the City of London. The fire began in Pudding Lane and quickly spread through the wooden buildings. Amazingly only

The Tower of London, William I's fortress, was also used as a royal palace and, particularly in Tudor times, as a notorious prison.

six people died, but 13,000 houses, 87 parish churches and St Paul's Cathedral were destroyed in the blaze.

Christopher Wren was appointed to oversee the rebuilding of London. His greatest work is St Paul's Cathedral. When he called for a stone to mark the centre of the site for the rebuilding, a workman picked up part of an old tombstone. On it was the word *Resurgam*, meaning 'I shall rise again'. The word came to symbolise not only the rebuilding of the cathedral, but the whole city.

Georgian London

By 1700 three-quarters of Londoners lived outside the old City, many in new fashionable suburbs in St James's, Soho, Mayfair and Holborn. Landowners capitalised on their assets by leasing out plots in large squares which still bear their names, for example, Leicester Square, Bedford Square and Russell Square.

Building continued towards Hyde Park with large houses such as Apsley House and

Somerset House was designed by William Chambers and built in the Strand, on the bank of the Thames, in the 1770s.

Burlington House (now the Royal Academy in Piccadilly). Two new bridges were erected across the Thames, at Westminster in 1750 and at Blackfriars in 1769.

Royal residences expanded. In 1689 William of Orange took over a house in Kensington and, with Sir Christopher Wren's help, made it into Kensington Palace. George III bought Buckingham Palace from the Duke of Buckingham and later his lavish son, George IV, engaged John Nash to redesign it.

Georgian London was a city of great contrasts. While Samuel Johnson entertained his contemporaries with conversation and wit, and businessmen met in coffee houses, Hogarth was recording the life of the poor in drawings such as 'Gin Lane'.

The Monument, close to the northern end of London Bridge, was designed by Wren to commemorate the Great Fire of 1666.

19th-century London

By the 1830s the Industrial Revolution was sweeping through London, changing it into a manufacturing centre as well as a trading city. The growing population spread out in all directions: poor workers crowded together around the docks and sweatshops of the East End, and wealthier people moved west into Kensington, Holland Park and Chelsea. The existing city also saw much new building, including Trafalgar Square and Shaftesbury Avenue. In 1834 the Houses of Parliament burned down and were rebuilt in their present Gothic style by Charles Barry and Augustus Pugin.

The first omnibus was introduced in 1829 and the first train steamed into London Bridge in 1836. Masses of clerks and factory workers moved out into newly built suburbs that now engulfed former villages, such as Hampstead, Highgate, Blackheath and Clapham. People from all over Britain poured into London through the main railway stations – Euston, Kings Cross and Paddington had opened by 1853, to be followed in the next two decades by Blackfriars, Charing Cross and St Pancras. In 1863, the world's first underground railway linked some of the main stations.

In 1851 Prince Albert, Queen Victoria's consort, arranged the Great Exhibition, centred around the magnificent Crystal Palace, a vast glass conservatory in which the achievements of Britain in science and technology were displayed to the world. The Exhibition was astoundingly successful, and the money it made was used to build the Royal Albert Hall, the Victoria and Albert Museum and other museums in Kensington.

Victorian London was at the heart of a worldwide empire. Goods from India, China and Africa were shipped up the Thames. Companies which bore the names of obscure and exotic places such as the River Plate, Hudson's Bay and Burma had their headquarters in the City, so that Freya Stark later said they created a 'feeling of being all over the world at once'.

The Midland Railway Company opened its London terminus at St Pancras in 1868.

Canary Wharf Tower, the tallest building in Britain, was built during the 1980s as part of a scheme to regenerate the decaying Docklands.

More than 6 million people visited the Crystal Palace in Hyde Park, the centre of Prince Albert's Great Exhibition of 1851.

20th century

The 20th century brought great changes to London. Before World War II, the steady expansion of buildings and people into outlying, leafier suburbs had been aided by the arrival of the motor car and more underground railway lines.

The war destroyed much of central London, including part of St Paul's Cathedral. Many of the modern buildings which arose on the bombsites were such characterless, concrete monstrosities, that Prince Charles claimed modern planners and architects had done more damage to London than the Luftwaffe. Architects learned from their mistakes and today exciting and innovative structures, such as the Lloyd's building, co-exist with old and historic buildings.

The advent of the new millennium generated a new wave of projects, particularly along the River Thames. River traffic had decreased rapidly during the second half of the century when ports lower down the Thames opened up to handle container ships and oil tankers. For decades abandoned warehouses and docks lined the river between Tower Bridge and Greenwich. Today a river walk links the graceful and breathtaking British Airways London Eye and the cultural complex of the South Bank with Tate Modern, Shakespeare's Globe and Tower Bridge. The path continues through 8 kilometres (5 miles) of regenerated docklands down to Greenwich and the Dome, although river cruises and a new tube line provide a faster route!

Buckingham Palace is the London home of Her Majesty Queen Elizabeth II. The palace was built for the Duke of Buckingham between 1703 and 1705, but in 1821 George IV commissioned the court architect, John Nash, to extend the building. The main eastern façade dates from 1913 and includes the balcony where members of the Royal Family appear on special occasions.

The Queen is guarded by five regiments of Foot Guards, in distinctive ceremonial dress with red jackets and tall bearskin hats. Large crowds gather to watch the ceremony of Changing the Guard. Here the Old Guard leaves St James's Palace on its way to Buckingham Palace.

Several of the State Rooms in Buckingham Palace are open to the public in the late summer, when these fabulous interiors and paintings by Vermeer, Rubens and Rembrandt can be seen.

The Royal Mews contains the coaches and cars used by Her Majesty the Queen. The sumptuous gilt coaches include the Gold State Coach used for coronations, the Irish State Coach and many others.

Kensington Palace was redesigned by Sir Christopher Wren and Nicholas Hawksmoor after William III bought the palace in 1689. Queen Victoria was born here but its most famous recent occupant was Diana, Princess of Wales. The palace is in Kensington Gardens, close to the Round Pond.

Westminster Abbey is probably the most historic church in Britain and the site for most royal coronations, weddings and burials since the 11th century. The two west towers were added in the 18th century.

The quire of Westminster Abbey and the sanctuary, where monarchs are crowned. Behind the high altar is St Edward's Chapel, which contains the impressively ornate tomb of Edward the Confessor. At the west end of the nave is a memorial to Winston Churchill and the Tomb of the Unknown Warrior, which commemorates the many thousands of unidentified soldiers killed in World War I.

Above the west door of Westminster Abbey are ten 20th-century martyrs, including St Elizabeth of Russia, Martin Luther King and Dietrich Bonhoeffer.

Westminster Abbey was refounded by King Edward the Confessor and consecrated in 1065, just a few days before he died. Edward the Confessor was later made a saint. This 20th-century stained-glass window in the nave is by Sir Ninian Comper.

The Lady Chapel in Westminster Abbey was built by Henry VII and contains the tombs of Henry and his wife, Elizabeth of York. The exquisite vaulting contains many royal emblems, including roses, fleurs-de-lis and portcullises.

Westminster Cathedral, off Victoria Street, is the main Roman Catholic church in England. It was completed in 1903, and its Italian-Byzantine architecture, with its saucer-shaped domes and tall campanile, is unique in London. The gallery at the top of the tower gives magnificent views.

The church of St Martin-in-the-Fields (below), in the north-east corner of Trafalgar Square, is named after the patron saint of beggars and houses a social care unit for those in need. In addition to services, the church holds regular free lunch-time classical concerts.

The church of St Bride's in Fleet Street is one of many designed by Sir Christopher Wren after the Great Fire of London in 1666. The church is known as 'the journalists' and printers' church', from the time when most of Britain's national newspapers had their offices in Fleet Street. In the crypt is a fascinating museum of the area since Roman times.

The tower and steeple of St Mary-le-Bow in Cheapside in the City are by Sir Christopher Wren, one of 51 City churches designed by this great architect. The grand interior of the church was rebuilt after a fire in 1941.

The interior of the church of St Stephen Walbrook (above) in the City is one of Sir Christopher Wren's most magnificent. The Samaritans, the organisation which befriends those contemplating suicide, was founded in the church in 1953.

The Norman church of St Bartholomew the Great in Smithfield is the oldest parish church in London. After the Reformation, parts of the church were used for other purposes, which included a printing works in the Lady Chapel where Benjamin Franklin once worked, but the choir retains the Norman arches and London's only medieval font.

St Paul's Cathedral is Sir Christopher Wren's great masterpiece. It was built of Portland stone over the ashes of the previous cathedral destroyed in the Great Fire of 1666. The cathedral is a magnificent example of baroque architecture, with one of the largest domes in the world.

The dome of St Paul's includes the famous Whispering Gallery – a message whispered onto the wall on one side can be heard on the opposite side. Paintings of the life of St Paul decorate the interior of the dome.

The quire of St Paul's has been the setting for many of the nation's great state occasions, including the funeral of Sir Winston Churchill in 1965 and the marriage of Prince Charles and Lady Diana Spencer in 1981.

Southwark Cathedral, hidden behind the warehouses on the south bank of the Thames, was built between 1213 and 1235 in the Early English Gothic style. The Harvard Chapel commemorates John Harvard, after whom the famous American university is named.

This monument to William Shakespeare is in Southwark Cathedral, close to Shakespeare's Globe Theatre.

The Houses of Parliament are the seat of national government. Elected members of Parliament meet in the Chamber of the House of Commons to debate government policies and vote on new laws. The House of Lords reviews the work of the House of Commons and suggests amendments. The buildings were designed by Charles Barry after the Palace of Westminster burnt down in 1834.

The clock tower of the Houses of Parliament contains the 13.5-tonne bell known as Big Ben and is one of London's best-known landmarks. Each minute hand is 4.2 metres (14 feet) long and the clock faces are 7 metres (23 feet) across.

No. 10 Downing Street has been the official residence of Britain's prime minister since it was offered to Robert Walpole in the 18th century. The street was developed by George Downing and was built on some of the remains of the royal Palace of Whitehall.

A statue of Sir Winston Churchill stands in Parliament Square, in front of the House of Commons. Churchill is best known for his leadership and for the stirring speeches he made to the nation during World War II.

Trafalgar Square was designed by John Nash to commemorate Admiral Lord Nelson's naval victory at the Battle of Trafalgar in 1805. The statue of Nelson stands on top of a 51-metre (167-foot) high column.

This charming statue of Charlie Chaplin stands in the garden in the centre of Leicester Square. It commemorates the famous tramp of silent cinema, which Charlie Chaplin created.

Trafalgar Square is a popular meeting place for tourists, revellers on New Year's Eve, political demonstrators – and pigeons.

Admiralty Arch, between Trafalgar Square and the Mall, was built in 1910 as a memorial to Queen Victoria. A few members of the government have secure lodgings here, close to Westminster.

The statue of Eros stands in the centre of Piccadilly Circus. Although Eros is the Greek god of love, the statue represents the angel of Christian charity and was erected in memory of Lord Shaftesbury, a 19th-century philanthropist.

The Savoy is one of several London hotels whose names have for decades been associated with top-class service to the rich and famous.

Traditional red telephone boxes stand outside the entrance to The Ritz, not for the benefit of guests, but for passers-by . . .

. . . who crowd the streets of central London.

Covent Garden, now a centre for crafts and fashionable shops, was London's main fruit and vegetable market until the 1970s when the market was moved out. The light, airy structure of the old market building gives plenty of space for restaurants, cafés and shops, while outside . . .

. . . buskers entertain shoppers and passers-by with a wide variety of street theatre, including mime, juggling and music.

Cumberland Terrace, on the edge of Regent's Park, is one of several elegant terraces designed by John Nash in 1812 for the Prince Regent (later George IV).

Apsley House at Hyde Park Corner was the home of the Duke of Wellington, the general who defeated Napoleon at the Battle of Waterloo, and is now the Wellington Museum. The house was built in the 1770s by Robert Adam and its address was simply 'No. 1 London'.

Gerrard Street, just north of Leicester Square, is at the heart of London's Chinatown. Here are oriental restaurants, Chinese supermarkets and other exotic shops.

Grosvenor Square in Mayfair, just one of London's many large, elegant squares, is bordered by the American Embassy on the west. The statue is of the American president, Franklin D. Roosevelt.

As London's summers have become warmer, bars, cafés and pubs have spilled out onto the pavements in quiet alleys, on street corners . . .

. . . and on Old Compton Street in Soho. This area, once open fields used for hunting, has been home to many immigrants, including Huguenots from France and refugees from Italy, Greece, China and Russia. Today the area has a cosmopolitan mix of shops, restaurants and patisseries.

Harrods is London's best-known department store. It was established in 1849 as a grocer's shop, but by 1894 Henry Harrod had made it world famous with the claim to supply 'all things to all people everywhere'. The store has even supplied Ronald Reagan with an Indian elephant! Interior decorations include Art Nouveau and Art Deco styles, such as these tiles in the Food Hall.

Oxford Street is London's most popular shopping street. Gordon Selfridge, a Chicago millionaire, opened Selfridges in 1909 as a store 'dedicated to the service of women'. It invited customers to 'spend a day at Selfridge's', not only to shop, but to have lunch and a hairdo.

Kensington Church Street is one of several streets and markets which specialise in antiques . . .

. . . and Portobello Road market is another. On Saturday mornings the market stretches from the antiques stalls at the southern end to the Westway flyover, where stalls sell vegetables, cheap clothes and other goods.

On Saturdays and Sundays, Camden Lock market is packed with stalls selling crafts and snacks from around the world. Here you may find jewellery from India, clothes from Indonesia, wooden carvings from Africa, jerseys from South America, together with goods made by the stall-holders.

One of London's lesser known markets is held in Columbia Road in the East End on Sunday mornings. Here plants and flowers are on sale for amazingly low prices.

Cecil Court, off Charing Cross Road, is a small alley of second-hand bookshops, ideal for a quiet browse. Charing Cross Road has many specialist bookshops as well as large, well-known stores, such as Foyles and Waterstones.

Savile Row in Mayfair is synonymous with top-quality, traditional men's tailors. Shoppers can buy ready-made clothes here, but they are expensive.

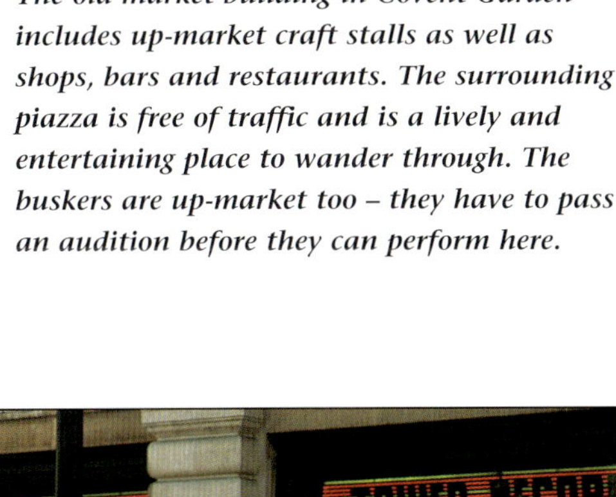

The old market building in Covent Garden includes up-market craft stalls as well as shops, bars and restaurants. The surrounding piazza is free of traffic and is a lively and entertaining place to wander through. The buskers are up-market too – they have to pass an audition before they can perform here.

You can get around London by tube or bus, or you can hail a cab. This taxi is a 'black cab' and is strictly regulated.

Tower of London

The Crown Jewels – the 'ornaments and jewels of the crown' – have been kept in the Tower of London since 1303. They include crowns, swords, precious gems and historic plate. The Imperial State Crown is decorated with 3,000 diamonds and the ruby worn by Henry V at the Battle of Agincourt.

The White Tower within the Tower of London was built by William the Conqueror to defend the city. Over the next 400 years the two protective walls, the other towers, and the Chapel of St Peter ad Vincula were added. Built as a fortress, the Tower has also served as a prison for many illustrious prisoners. The 'Little Princes' – Edward V and his brother Richard – were mysteriously murdered here.

Ravens help to guard the Tower of London. It is said that if the ravens ever leave, the White Tower will fall and a great disaster befall the kingdom. Just to make sure that no such catastrophe occurs, the ravens' wings are clipped!

Many people who entered the Tower through Traitors' Gate (above) never saw the outside world again. Catherine Howard, Henry VIII's fifth wife, was brought through here in 1542 and executed just a few days later.

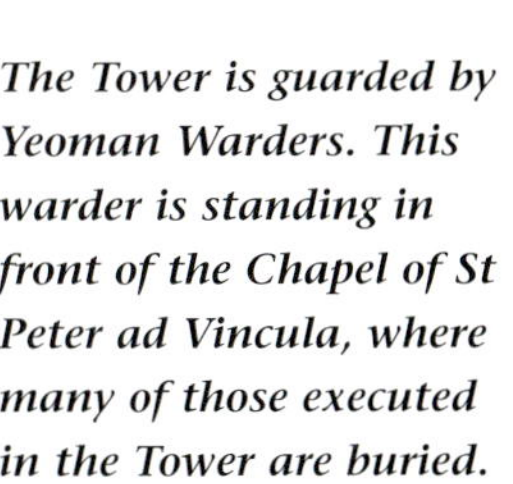

The Tower is guarded by Yeoman Warders. This warder is standing in front of the Chapel of St Peter ad Vincula, where many of those executed in the Tower are buried.

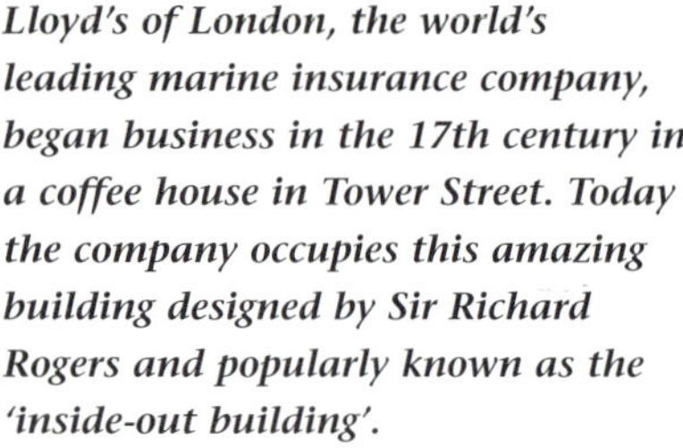

Lloyd's of London, the world's leading marine insurance company, began business in the 17th century in a coffee house in Tower Street. Today the company occupies this amazing building designed by Sir Richard Rogers and popularly known as the 'inside-out building'.

Several dragons mark the boundary of the City, which retains a remarkable amount of independence from the rest of London. The City has, for example, its own police force and its own Lord Mayor.

The City's international financial power rests on centuries of tradition. The Royal Exchange (below), founded by Sir Thomas Gresham in the 16th century, is the third building on this site. The Bank of England (on the left of the photo) was set up in 1694. One of its main roles today is to stabilise the country's economy by setting interest rates.

Skyscraper office blocks dominate the City's skyline, with the dome of St Paul's Cathedral the sole survivor from an earlier age. The City is the financial centre of Britain and the home of several international financial markets.

Ye Olde Cheshire Cheese pub (left), hidden in an alleyway off Fleet Street, was said to be a favourite haunt of Dr Samuel Johnson. It is one of London's genuinely old and quaint pubs.

Greenwich

The Royal Observatory in Greenwich Park was set up by Charles II in the 17th century to plot the stars in an attempt to solve the problem of measuring longitude at sea. Greenwich later became the marker of the prime meridian – longitude zero – and the line is marked in red on the courtyard inside the Observatory.

Greenwich Park stretches up the hill behind the National Maritime Museum to the Royal Observatory and Blackheath beyond. The Queen's House, now in the centre of the Museum, was designed by architect Inigo Jones for James I's queen, Anne of Denmark. On the riverbank is the Royal Naval College.

Down river from Greenwich is the world's largest dome, one of London's newest landmarks. The Dome was built to celebrate the millennium in the year 2000 and opened with exhibits which included breath-taking trapeze acts and different aspects of human achievement.

The Cutty Sark*, a 19th-century tea clipper, lies in a dry dock near Greenwich pier. This graceful sailing ship once raced across the Indian Ocean with her cargo of the new season's tea, and later with wool from Australia. Clippers lost the race to steam-ships when the Suez Canal was opened in 1869, but their historic past is preserved in the museum on board the ship.*

The National Maritime Museum charts the history of ships and shipping, both peaceful and naval. It includes boats, paintings and cannons among its exhibits, as well as many interactive displays and this charming figurehead of Seringapatay.

The Prospect of Whitby in Wapping dates from 1520 and is probably London's oldest pub. J.M.W. Turner and James Whistler both painted the river from its terrace. Today this tiny riverside pub is much enjoyed by tourists.

The River Thames has played an essential part in London's life since the city was founded by the Romans. It was a highway for people and for goods; today cruise boats take tourists from central London to Greenwich and Hampton Court.

Tower Bridge, one of London's most famous landmarks, was opened in 1894. Its Gothic towers were designed to fit in with the architecture of the Tower of London nearby. About 500 times a year its Victorian hydraulic engines lift the bascules carrying the roadway to allow tall ships to pass through.

Many old docks and warehouses have been rejuvenated as shops, offices and luxury apartments. Hay's Wharf, where tea, coffee and butter were once unloaded and stored, has been converted into Hay's Galleria – a complex of shops, cafés and offices. In the middle, a water feature called The Navigators occasionally sprays unsuspecting passers-by.

Until the middle of the 20th century, the Thames was lined with docks and warehouses up to and beyond Tower Bridge. Now huge container ships load and unload further down the river, leaving the old docks redundant. St Katherine's Dock, close to the Tower of London, has been converted into a fashionable marina.

British Airways London Eye undoubtedly gives the best views of London. It is the highest viewing platform in London and carries passengers 135 metres (450 feet) into the air for stunning views of the city and, on a clear day, to the countryside beyond.

Although called Cleopatra's Needle because it stood outside Cleopatra's palace in Alexandria, this Egyptian obelisk dates back to 1450 BC. It was brought to London in 1878 and erected on the recently built Embankment.

The two sphinxes which were intended to be guardians of Cleopatra's Needle were positioned the wrong way round – they face inwards instead of outwards!

The lamps on Westminster Bridge bear the monogram V and A, after Queen Victoria and her consort Prince Albert. The bridge was opened in 1863 with a 25-gun salute, one for each year that the Queen had reigned.

Lambeth Palace, opposite the Houses of Parliament, has been the London residence of the Archbishop of Canterbury since the 12th century, although the present building, apart from the Tudor entrance tower, dates mainly from the 19th century.

HMS Belfast*, a cruiser from World War II, is now a floating naval museum. The ship played a leading role in destroying the German battle cruiser* Scharnhorst*, and in the Normandy landings.*

The Thames is tidal as far as Richmond and beyond. At high tide parts of the riverside walk are under water. In the past Henry VIII and his court sailed by barge up the Thames . . .

. . . to his palace at Hampton Court. Henry acquired the palace from Thomas Wolsey, his Lord Chancellor, when he fell out of favour with the King. Henry proceeded to spend a vast sum of money enlarging Wolsey's already magnificent palace. There is much to see at Hampton Court, including the Tudor kitchens and the famous maze.

London's Chinese community celebrates Chinese New Year in colourful style. Each year, in January or February, a procession of dragons and other exotic creatures takes to the streets, watched by delighted Londoners.

Every May the extensive gardens of the Royal Hospital in Chelsea are taken over for the Chelsea Flower Show. Gardeners flock from across the country to enjoy the amazing blooms and displays, and even the on-duty police cannot resist their charms!

The London Marathon, held each April, brings thousands of people onto the streets – and they are just the runners. Thousands of spectators line the route from Greenwich to Tower Bridge, through the East End to finish in Westminster. Competitors include serious runners, competitors in wheelchairs and those having fun raising money for charity.

The colourful Trooping the Colour takes place in early June to celebrate the Queen's official birthday. The Queen inspects her personal troops on Horse Guards Parade before watching a display of marching to the music of massed bands.

Wimbledon's grass tennis courts provide some of the fastest and most exciting tennis in the world. In late June, tennis fans are glued to their television screens as they watch the best players compete to become champion, but, for those lucky enough to get tickets, there is nothing to beat Wimbledon's incomparable atmosphere – and strawberries.

The State Opening of Parliament is one of London's great royal ceremonies. After a State procession from Buckingham Palace to the Houses of Parliament, the Queen reads out the legislation which the government plans to introduce in the next session.

On the last weekend in August, the streets of Notting Hill reverberate to the sound of the Notting Hill Carnival – a hugely noisy and colourful street party organised by London's West Indian community. The spectacular floats and amazing costumes are the result of a year's careful work.

The City of London has its own mayor who is elected each year. In November the new mayor is installed at a ceremony at the Law Courts. The pageant, called the Lord Mayor's Show, begins with a procession through the City from Mansion House to the Law Courts and ends with a fireworks display over the River Thames.

The British Museum is one of the world's greatest museums. It has sculptures and artefacts from all the major ancient civilisations. Treasures include the Rosetta Stone, which helped to break the code of Egyptian hieroglyphs, the Elgin Marbles from the Parthenon in Athens, Egyptian mummies and exquisite Chinese vases.

The history of scientific discovery and achievements from early inventions to space technology is celebrated at the Science Museum. Many displays are interactive and are particularly popular with children.

The Natural History Museum is one of several museums in South Kensington. Exhibits display thousands of animals and plants, living and extinct, including the reconstructed skeletons of Diplodocus, other immense dinosaurs and a Blue whale – the largest animal that has ever lived.

The Lord Mayor's coach, used every year in the Lord Mayor's Show, is on display for the rest of the year at the Museum of London, part of the Barbican complex in the City. The museum traces the history of London from prehistoric times to the present day.

This beautiful box is the Becket Casket, made to hold relics of St Thomas à Becket, the 12th-century archbishop of Canterbury assassinated during the reign of Henry II. It can be seen in the Victoria and Albert Museum, a museum of the decorative arts which includes furniture, jewellery, costume and glassware.

Madame Tussaud inherited her original collection of waxworks from her uncle in France. She came to London in 1802 and opened a museum near Baker Street in 1835. Her figures include the rich and famous, and the macabre – the chamber of horrors has always been a popular feature of the collection.

Jan van Eyck's exquisite and intriguing painting known as The Arnolfini Marriage *hangs in the National Gallery in Trafalgar Square. The gallery displays the work of great masters, such as Vincent Van Gogh, Rubens, Caravaggio, Titian and Leonardo da Vinci.*

Eduardo Paolozzi's dramatic statue of Newton stands outside the British Library in Euston Road. The Library's treasures on display to the public include Shakespeare's First Folio and the Magna Carta, as well as other original manuscripts, musical scores and book illustrations.

Turner's Burning of the Houses of Parliament *is one of many paintings by this famous British artist, whose work takes pride of place in Tate Britain on Millbank. The gallery, founded in 1897 by Henry Tate, the sugar magnate, now displays British art including works by Hogarth, Reynolds, Gainsborough and Constable.*

Tate Modern displays works of modern art in a magnificent building, which was once a power station, on the south bank of the River Thames. Here you can see paintings and sculptures by such 20th-century masters as Matisse, Kandinsky, Henry Moore and Pablo Picasso.

The Royal Opera House in Covent Garden is the home of the Royal Opera and Royal Ballet companies. Many famous artists have performed in this magnificent building.

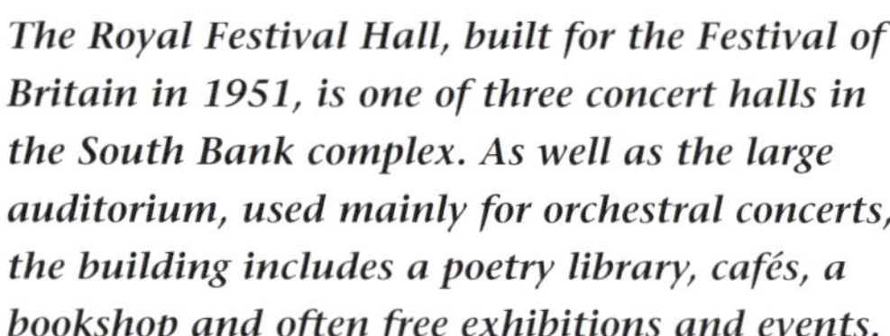

The Royal Festival Hall, built for the Festival of Britain in 1951, is one of three concert halls in the South Bank complex. As well as the large auditorium, used mainly for orchestral concerts, the building includes a poetry library, cafés, a bookshop and often free exhibitions and events.

London has not one but three venues for international ballet – the Royal Opera House, Sadlers Wells and the London Coliseum. Here Stravinsky's The Firebird *is performed at the London Coliseum near Trafalgar Square.*

The Theatre Royal in Drury Lane was a favourite venue of Charles II, who came here to see his mistress Nell Gwynne on stage. She was one of the first women to 'tread the boards' – previously women's roles had been played by young men. The present theatre is now used for blockbuster musicals.

Shakespeare's Globe Theatre is a reconstruction of the theatre where Julius Caesar *and many of William Shakespeare's other plays were first performed between 1599 and 1612. The present theatre was the inspiration of Sam Wanamaker and copies the original, not only in design but in building methods and materials too.*

Parks and Gardens

The Serpentine is a haven for waterbirds and people seeking a leisurely time afloat. On New Year's Day hardy bathers break the ice if necessary to enjoy a traditional swim.

London is remarkable for its many royal parks and wide expanses of grass and trees, even in the centre of the city. The Serpentine is a large lake that links Hyde Park to Kensington Gardens making the largest open space in central London.

The colourful Queen Mother's Gate, Hyde Park.

This charming statue of J.M. Barrie's famous character, Peter Pan, was commissioned in 1911 and erected overnight in Kensington Gardens so that it appeared as if by magic.

Two memorials to Prince Albert, the husband whom Queen Victoria adored. The statue in Kensington Gardens shows him with the catalogue for the Great Exhibition of 1851. The Royal Albert Hall behind is the main venue for the Henry Wood Promenade concerts, held every summer.

St James's Park provides a welcome escape from the noise and traffic. Tourists and Londoners come to relax, to feed the ducks, listen to the band and enjoy the beautiful flowers. St James's Park was once the private estate of St James's Palace on the other side of the Mall.

Green Park, between Buckingham Palace and Piccadilly, looks best in spring when thousands of daffodils carpet the grass.

Huge, ancient trees shade the grass in Lincoln's Inn, one of the four Inns of Court which lie between the West End and the City. Here barristers and law students receive and prepare briefs.

Soho Square was one of the first 18th-century squares. On warm days every patch of grass in central London is invaded by office workers at lunchtime. Pigeons, however, are on the lookout for scraps at all times of the day!

London Zoo, home to more than 12,000 animals from around the world, prides itself on its work on conservation and with endangered species. These lion tamarins are two of its many rare species.

Regent's Park was once one of Henry VIII's hunting grounds. Today its beautiful rose gardens, football pitches and outdoor theatre are enjoyed by thousands. On the west side of the park is London's central, gold-domed mosque, while in the north-east corner is London Zoo.

Hampstead Heath in north London consists of many acres of enclosed and rolling parkland. It includes woods, open-air swimming in several ponds, kite-flying and a magnificent view of London from the top of Parliament Hill.

Giant water lilies in the Royal Botanic Gardens at Kew, one of the most famous collections of plants and trees in the world. Plants from the rainforest to the desert grow in grand conservatories, each with its own microclimate, while trees from around the world thrive in the gardens outside.

The Chinese pagoda, commissioned by Princess Augusta, in Kew Gardens. The Princess began the gardens with the help of Joseph Banks, the botanist who accompanied Captain Cook on his first voyage to Australia.

Famous Londoners

Charles Dickens recreates the people and streets of Victorian London in books such as Little Dorrit, Great Expectations, Bleak House *and* Our Mutual Friend. *His home at 47 Doughty Street in Holborn is now the Dickens House Museum.*

Samuel Johnson famously said 'The man who is tired of London is tired of life.' His statue stands between Fleet Street and the Strand, between the City and the West End. In the 18th century Johnson – essayist, poet, conversationalist, and compiler of the first major dictionary of the English language – was at the centre of London's literary and intellectual life.

Samuel Pepys, whose monument is in St Olave's church in the City, kept a diary from 1 January 1660 until May 1669. He witnessed and recorded the Restoration of King Charles II, the Great Plague and the Great Fire of London. His diaries, which were never intended for publication, also reveal details of his personal life, including his many affairs with mistresses.

William Hogarth, the great satirical and moral artist, depicted the seamier side of London life in the 18th century, including 'Gin Lane' which showed the deprivations of poverty and alcohol. In 1735 Hogarth founded an academy of art in St Martin's Lane, the most important art school in London until the Royal Academy was established.

The legend of Dick Whittington tells how the chimes of Bow Bells stopped him leaving London: 'Turn again, Whittington, thrice Lord Mayor of London,' they seemed to predict. Richard Whittington made his fortune as a cloth merchant in London and became Lord Mayor four times. He founded various charitable institutions and left money to pave the new Guildhall.

The Sherlock Holmes pub is a shrine to Sir Arthur Conan Doyle's great fictional detective. In the short stories, Sherlock Holmes and his assistant Watson live at 221B Baker Street, and, 100 years later, people still write to that address in the hope of enlisting his help in solving difficult cases!

London at Night

The outside of the London IMAX Cinema at Waterloo looks almost as impressive as the vast screen inside showing two- and three-dimensional films.

The West End is crammed with theatres. Some productions run for months . . .

. . . others for years . . .

. . . while the record-beating play The Mousetrap *has been running continuously since 1952.*

London is just as lively at night as it is during the day. The South Bank throngs with concert- and theatre-goers, who enjoy not only the performances but also the floodlit view of the river.

Many famous landmarks are floodlit at night. The inspiration for Marble Arch, at the junction of Oxford Street, Park Lane and Bayswater, came from the Arch of Constantine in Rome.

Piccadilly Circus is at the hub of London's nightlife. Electronic advertisements add to the bright lights and exciting atmosphere. Whatever your taste, London has plenty to offer.

At Christmas the city of Oslo gives London a vast fir tree which is set up in Trafalgar Square and becomes the focus for Christmas celebrations.

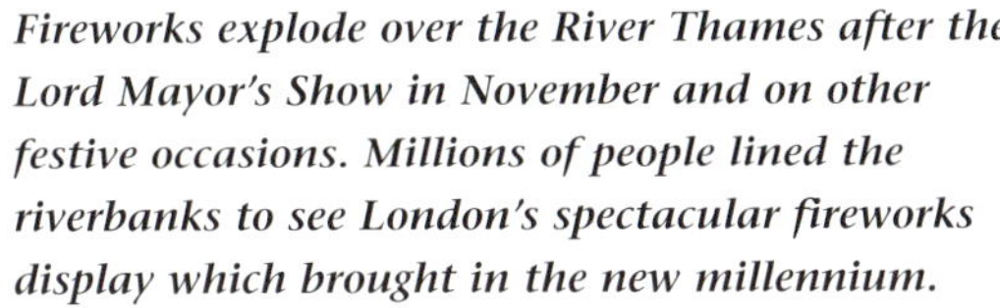

Fireworks explode over the River Thames after the Lord Mayor's Show in November and on other festive occasions. Millions of people lined the riverbanks to see London's spectacular fireworks display which brought in the new millennium.

Index